THE

# RULES

OF THE

# Tavern Club

OF

# BOSTON.

## WITH A LIST OF THE OFFICERS & MEMBERS.

*Meum est propositum in Taberna mori.*

BOSTON:
PRINTED FOR The Tavern Club
MCMXI.

SEAL OF THE TAVERN C

HENRY MORSE STEPHENS

OFFICERS OF

# The Tavern Club

## FOR THE YEAR
### 1911–12

President
HENRY LEE HIGGINSON

Vice-Presidents
ARLO BATES
ROBERT GRANT

Secretary
HOLKER ABBOTT

Treasurer
HENRY GOODWIN VAUGHAN

Directors
WALTER CHANNING BAILEY
CHARLES KIMBALL CUMMINGS
JOHN WHEELOCK ELLIOT
WILLIAM JAMES
WILLIAM STANLEY PARKER
ARTHUR STANWOOD PIER
GEORGE BAXTER UPHAM, *Chairman*

3

## Officers

### Election Committee

HOLKER ABBOTT
SAMUEL CABOT
CHARLES STEWART FORBES
MARK ANTONY DE WOLFE HOWE
GUY LOWELL
·HENRY LYMAN
PAUL THORNDIKE
ELIOT WADSWORTH
LANGDON WARNER
ARTHUR HENRY WEED

### House Committee

GUY MURCHIE .
CHARLES STEWART FORBES
PAUL THORNDIKE

## Club House

### No. 4 BOYLSTON PLACE

# THE RULES OF
# Ⓣⱨe Ⓣavern Club

## I
## Name

THIS Club shall be called Ⓣⱨe Ⓣavern Club, and is established for dining and social purposes.

## II
## Members

The number of active members of the Club shall be limited to one hundred and twenty-five, in addition to the President, Vice-Presidents, Treasurer, Secretary, and Chairman of the House Committee.

Whenever any person shall be proposed for membership, written application shall be made by a member of the Club to the Secretary, and his name shall be submitted to the Committee on Elections.

It shall be the duty of the Secretary to mail to the active members of the Club, at least three weeks before any regular meeting of the Committee on Elections, a notice marked "confidential," which shall contain the names of all candidates who are to be considered at that meeting, and no action shall be taken on any candidate by the Committee on Elections, unless his name shall have been placed before the active members of the Club in this manner and unless, in the case of candidates for active membership, he be known personally to at least four members of the Committee.

Members may communicate in writing, through the Secretary, their opinion for or against any candidate, and these communications shall be laid before the Committee on Elections, and shall be considered as confidential.

Six members of the Committee on Elections shall constitute a quorum, and the unanimous consent of all present shall be required to admit any candidate to membership in the Club, and no candidate who has been rejected shall be considered again within six months.

# Rules of the Club

## III

## Government

The officers of the Club shall be a President, Treasurer, Secretary, and six Directors, who shall constitute the Executive Committee of the Club. Also, a Committee on Elections of nine in addition to the Secretary.

There shall also be two Vice-Presidents, whose duties shall be to preside at the social meetings of the Club in the absence of the President.

All such officers shall be elected, except as hereinafter provided, by ballot at the Annual Meeting, and they shall hold office for one year, and until their respective successors are elected, and each year at least two directors shall be elected who have not served on this Committee for the previous year.

The President shall, if present, preside at all meetings of the Club and of the Executive Committee.

The President and Vice-Presidents shall be exempt from paying the annual assessment.

If the office of President, of either of the Vice-Presidents, or of Treasurer shall become vacant, the Executive Committee shall call a special meeting of the Club to fill such vacancy for the remainder of the year. Other vacancies may be filled for the remainder of the year by the Executive Committee.

Any officer may be removed by the Club for misconduct.

Not less than four weeks previous to the Annual Meeting, the President shall appoint a committee of three, whose duty it shall be to nominate officers for the ensuing year. Said Committee shall report to the Secretary, who shall post in the Club a list of the nominations not less than two weeks previous to the annual meeting.

## IV

## Executive Committee

The Executive Committee shall, subject to the direction of the Club, have the entire management and control of the Club and of its affairs and property, except as provided in Rule XVIII; but they shall have no power to make the Club liable for indebtedness beyond the

8

amount of money which shall at the time of contracting the same be in the Treasurer's hands, and not needed for the discharge of prior debts and liabilities.

They may appoint from their number or from the members of the Club a House Committee, and such other Committees as they may deem necessary for the proper management of the affairs of the Club, and appoint their duties.

The chairman of the House Committee shall be exempt from paying the annual assessment.

## V

## Committee on Elections

The Committee on Elections shall consist of nine members, in addition to the Secretary, and they shall have full powers over the election of members. They shall be elected by the Club or appointed by the Executive Committee before September 1, 1905.

At its first meeting the Committee on Elections shall divide its members, not including the Secretary, by lot or otherwise, into three classes of three each; the term of office of the first class to expire at the Annual Meeting in 1906, of the second class at the same time in 1907, and of the third class at the same time in 1908. At each Annual Meeting after that of 1905, three new members of the Committee shall be chosen for the term of three years, and the members whose term of office expires shall not be eligible for re-election in the same year.

The Committee on Elections shall hold five meetings each year, — one in October, one in December, one in February, one in April, and one in June, and no action shall be taken on candidates proposed for membership at any other meetings. They shall also hold preliminary meetings at least one month before each regular meeting, to decide the candidates who are to be acted on at the regular meeting following.

If there should be no vacancies in the Club membership, or if there should be no candidates awaiting the decision of the Committee, it shall not be obliged to meet.

# VI

## Treasurer

The Treasurer shall be charged with the collection of dues, and the custody of the funds of the Club and their disbursement under the direction of the Executive Committee or of the Club. His accounts shall always be open to the inspection of the Executive Committee, and he shall present a yearly financial report at the Annual Meeting.

He shall be exempt from paying the annual assessment.

# VII

## Secretary

The Secretary shall call all meetings of the Club and of the Executive and Election Committees, and shall keep a record of all such meetings. He shall have the custody of all the documents of the Club, and shall conduct its correspondence.

He shall be exempt from paying the annual assessment.

# VIII
## Meetings of the Club

The Annual Meeting of the Club for the choice of officers and such other business as may properly come before it shall be held on the first Monday of May at eight o'clock P. M. or on any other date that the Executive Committee may select between April 25 and May 20.

Special meetings may be called at any time by order of the Executive Committee, and shall be called at the written request of seven members.

Notice of all meetings shall, five days at least previous thereto, be posted in the rooms of the Club, and sent by mail to the address of each member.

Fifteen members shall constitute a quorum, except for the purpose of passing amendments to the Rules of the Club, for which twenty-five members shall be necessary to constitute a quorum.

# IX
## Assessments

All persons elected to active membership shall pay an initiation fee of fifty dollars.

# Rules of the Club

There shall be an annual assessment of one hundred dollars upon active members, payable as follows: fifty dollars on the first day of April, and fifty dollars on the first day of October. The first payment shall be credited to the members respectively on their restaurant accounts, and they shall be required to pay no restaurant bills for the current fiscal year, April 1 to March 31, so long as any part of such credits shall remain unused. But all of such credits remaining unused at the end of the current fiscal year shall become the property of the Club.

All members elected after April first shall pay a proportionate part of the annual assessment for the year, from the first of the month following their election, and active members shall be entitled to a *pro rata* amount of credit at the restaurant for the current fiscal year.

Any active member who is absent from the United States for a year shall not be assessed more than thirty-five dollars for such year. And any active member who is so absent for six months or more, but less than a year, shall not be assessed more than fifty dollars for such year.

## X

## Payment of Dues

All indebtedness of members to the Club other than for assessments shall be paid on or before the first day of the month succeeding that in which it is contracted. And if at the expiration of the fourteenth day of any month any member shall not have paid the dues for the preceding month, he shall receive no further credit until such dues are paid.

It shall be the duty of the Secretary upon the fifteenth day of every month to post in some conspicuous place in the Club House the names of all members whose dues are then unpaid, together with the amount due from each, and cause the same to remain until they are paid.

## XI

## Forfeiture of Membership

The privileges of any member may, after due notice and specification of charges and hearing thereon, be suspended for cause by a two-thirds vote of the Executive Committee. Any such member may appeal from the action of the Committee to the Club, and a meeting of the Club shall thereupon be called by the Executive Committee to consider his appeal.

If two thirds of the members present at such meeting shall reverse the action of the Committee, the privileges of the suspended member shall be restored.

At any meeting of the Club called by the Executive Committee for the purpose of considering charges against a member, notice shall be addressed to the member affected at least one month previous to the holding thereof, and his membership may thereupon be forfeited by a two-thirds vote of the members present.

Any member whose assessment shall remain unpaid for a period of thirty days shall be notified by the Treasurer of the fact, and if, at the expiration of fifteen days thereafter, the assessment shall still remain unpaid, he shall thereby cease to be a member, subject to reinstatement by the Executive Committee for due cause.

A forfeiture of membership so made, either by the Club or by the Executive Committee, shall operate to deprive the member expelled of all right in the property and assets of the Club.

## XII

## Injury to Property

Any destruction of, or injury to, the property of the Club shall be paid for by the member who has caused the same.

# Rules of the Club

## XIII

## Servants

No member or visitor shall give any money or gratuity to any servant of the Club, or employ him on private business outside the Club, except with the consent of some member of the Executive Committee.

## XIV

## Visitors

All persons not members of the Club who reside forty miles or more beyond the limits of the city of Boston, and have no place of business therein, shall be deemed strangers.

The Executive Committee may extend the privilege of the Club House to any stranger during his visit to the city, but not for a period exceeding one month.

Any member may introduce a stranger into the Club House for the period of one week, with the consent of any member of the Executive Committee, and may introduce a stranger for one day without such consent.

Other persons not members may be introduced into the Club House not oftener than once in each month.

The names of all persons not members who are introduced into the Club House shall be registered in a book kept in the office of the Club, with the name of the member introducing them, and the date of the introduction.

No guest shall have the right to bring any person into the Club House, and the Executive Committee shall have the right at any time to exclude all persons not members.

Any member introducing a guest shall be responsible for all bills incurred by such guest.

## XV

## Non-Resident Members

In addition to the active members of the Club, persons residing forty miles or more from Boston, and having no place of business in Boston, may be elected as non-resident members.

Such members shall be elected in the

same way and have the same privileges as active members, except that they shall not be allowed to vote at business meetings or to propose candidates for membership.  ·

They shall pay an initiation fee of fifty dollars and an annual assessment of twenty-five dollars.

The number of such members shall never exceed sixty.

Officers of the army and navy may be considered as non-resident members.

An active member who shall cease to reside within forty miles of Boston, and shall remove his place of business from Boston, may at any time, at his own request and with the approval of the Executive Committee, become a non-resident member, unless the list of non-resident members is full.

If any non-resident member transfers his residence to within forty miles of Boston, or his place of business to Boston, he shall, as soon as a vacancy occurs in the active-membership list, be required to resign his non-resident membership.  His name shall then come before the Committee on Elections in the same manner as other candidates for active membership.

If elected, the sums already paid by him for initiation fee and annual assessment for the current year shall be deducted from the amount to be paid by him as an active member.

Any non-resident member elected previous to June 2, 1890, on transferring his place of residence to within forty miles of Boston, or his place of business to Boston, shall resign his non-resident membership as above provided, and shall become an active member, with the approval of the Executive Committee, and without any vote of the Club.

Any active member who has become at his own request a non-resident member, and who shall return to reside or to have a place of business in Boston or within forty miles of Boston, shall be entitled to resume his active membership, upon the approval of the Executive Committee, when a vacancy occurs.

## XVI

## Honorary Members

Honorary members shall be elected in the same manner as active members. They shall be eligible to no offices except those of President and Vice-President; and no honorary member, unless holding one of these offices, shall participate in business meetings. Honorary members shall not propose candidates for membership in the Club, nor vote on the election of members, but with the above exceptions shall have all the privileges of active members.

They shall be exempt from paying the initiation fee and the annual assessment.

## XVII

## Amendments

These rules may be amended at any meeting of the Club at which at least twenty-five members are present, with the assent of two thirds of those present, provided that a written notice of the proposed amendment is sent by the Secretary with the call for the meeting, and a copy of such notice is also posted in the Club House ten days at least previous to the meeting.

## XVIII

## Real Estate

The legal title to all real estate acquired for the Club shall be held by trustees, to be appointed by the Club, upon such trusts as the Club may determine.

## LIST OF MEMBERS

OF

# The Tavern Club

## SEPTEMBER, 1911

## Active Members

1885.  Holker Abbott
1896.  Winthrop Ames
1884.  Robert Day Andrews
1894.  Robert Whitman Atkinson
1884.  Francis Henry Bacon
1902.  Walter Channing Bailey
1892.  George Pierce Baker
1893.  Franklin Greene Balch
1904.  Francis Bartlett
1888.  Arlo Bates
1892.  Frank Weston Benson
1899.  Henry Forbes Bigelow
1894.  Joseph Smith Bigelow
1887.  William Sturgis Bigelow
1910.  Gerald Blake
1902.  John Bapst Blake
1884.  William Payne Blake
1896.  Dwight Blaney

# The Tavern Club

1887. Vincent Yardley Bowditch
1884. Edward Hickling Bradford
1901. George Washington Wales
   Brewster
1884. William Norton Bullard
1884. Harry Burnett
1887. Arthur Tracy Cabot
1907. Samuel Cabot
1909. George Whitfield Chadwick
1885. Heman White Chaplin
1908. Frederick Codman Cobb
1899. John Sturgis Codman
1899. Frederick Shepherd Converse
1890. John Templeman Coolidge, Jr.
1896. Charles Kimball Cummings
1892. Francis Gardner Curtis
1884. Hayward Warren Cushing
1884. Francis Henry Davenport
1893. Lorin Fuller Deland
1887. Richard Cowell Dixey
1904. George Buckman Dorr
1887. John Wheelock Elliot
1910. William Crowninshield Endicott
1907. Arthur Fairbanks
1908. John Wells Farley
1911. Whitcomb Field

# List of Members

1884. Reginald Heber Fitz
1907. Arthur Foote
1907. Charles Stewart Forbes
1884. James Goldthwaite Freeman
1884. Ignaz Marcel Gaugengigl
1889. Frederick Lewis Gay
1906. Wallace Goodrich
1888. Robert Grant
1901. Henry Copley Greene
1888. Curtis Guild, Jr.
1897. Charles Sumner Hamlin
1886. Augustus Hemenway
1899. Arthur Dehon Hill
1908. Richard Bryant Hobart
1897. Charles Hopkinson
1893. Mark Antony DeWolfe Howe
1887. Eliot Hubbard
1900. Byron Satterlee Hurlbut
1884. Frank Jackson
1911. Henry James, Jr.
1908. William James
1884. Herbert Jaques
1884. Clayton Johns
1888. Horatio Appleton Lamb
1884. Samuel Wood Langmaid
1906. Gardiner Martin Lane

25

1884. Elliot Cabot Lee
1884. Francis Wilson Lee
1909. John Torrey Linzee
1885. Charles Martin Loeffler
1888. Alexander Wadsworth Longfellow
1887. Robert Williamson Lovett
1894. Abbott Lawrence Lowell
1904. Frederick Eldredge Lowell
1900. Guy Lowell
1888. John Lowell, Jr.
1884. John Dandridge Henly Luce
1893. Matthew Luce
1892. Fred Bates Lund
1903. Henry Lyman
1910. Richard Cockburn Maclaurin
1884. John Hildreth McCollum
1890. Josiah Byram Millet
1884. George Howard Monks
1911. John Farwell Moore
1891. Edward Sylvester Morse
1886. Henry Lee Morse
1899. Guy Murchie
1904. Frederick Law Olmsted
1886. William Lincoln Parker
1904. William Stanley Parker
1902. William Samuel Patten

# List of Members

1905. Bliss Perry
1905. Andrew James Peters
1901. Arthur Stanwood Pier
1894. Bela Lyon Pratt
1884. Morton Prince
1891. Edward Reynolds
1884. William Lambert Richardson
1903. James Ford Rhodes
1885. Henry Munroe Rogers
1908. Sullivan Amory Sargent
1910. Ellery Sedgwick
1886. Frederick Cheever Shattuck
1903. Jeremiah Smith, Jr.
1884. Henry Harrison Sprague
1884. Charles Wilkins Sturgis
1884. Francis Shaw Sturgis
1890. Richard Clipston Sturgis
1884. Thomas Russell Sullivan
1892. Edmund Charles Tarbell
1909. William Roscoe Thayer
1890. Paul Thorndike
1884. George Baxter Upham
1901. Henry Goodwin Vaughan
1907. Eliot Wadsworth
1884. Oliver Fairfield Wadsworth
1910. Philip Wadsworth

# The Tavern Club

1911. Richard Goodwin Wadsworth
1887. Charles Howard Walker
1909. Langdon Warner
1902. Edward Ross Warren
1884. Francis Sedgwick Watson
1909. Arthur Henry Weed
1887. Barrett Wendell
1885. Franz Eduard Zerrahn

## Non-Resident Members

1887. Gorham Bacon, *New York*
1894. Wilder Dwight Bancroft, *Ithaca, New York*
1899. George Edward Barton, *Colorado Springs, Colorado*
1911. Robert Perkins Bass, *Peterborough, New Hampshire*
1909. Ernest Harold Baynes, *Meriden, New Hampshire*
1900. Gordon Knox Bell, *New York*
1906. Louis Sherrill Bigelow, *New York*
1887. Isidore Braggiotti, *Florence, Italy*
1905. Walter Kirkpatrick Brice, *New York*
1896. Francis Henry Balfour Byrne, *New York*

# List of Members

1909. John Jay Chapman, *New York*

1900. Winston Churchill, *Windsor, Vermont*

1899. Walter John Clemson, *Taunton, Massachusetts*

1906. James Freeman Curtis, *Washington*

1897. Howard Gardiner Cushing, *New York*

1896. Theodore Montgomery Davis, *Newport, Rhode Island*

1889. Reginald De Koven, *New York*

1895. Carroll Dunham, *Irvington-on-Hudson, New York*

1884. Edward Kellogg Dunham, *New York*

1884. Henry Strong Durand, *Rochester, New York*

1889. Frank Duveneck, *Covington, Kentucky*

1900. Franklin Goodridge Fessenden, *Greenfield, Massachusetts*

1896. Arthur Lyman Fiske, *New York*

1905. Horace Fletcher, *Venice, Italy*

1899. William Cameron Forbes, *Philippines*

1898. Bertram Grosvenor Goodhue, *New York*

1902. Russell Hubbard Greeley, *Paris, France*

1909. John Hayes Hammond, *New York*

1909. Clarence Hay, *Newbury, New Hampshire*

1891. Harrison Blake Hodges, *New York*

1900. James Hazen Hyde, *New York*

1884. Eustace Jaques, *Lenox, Massachusetts*

1906. Marshall Rutgers Kernochan, *New York*

1895. Lincoln Newton Kinnicutt, *Worcester, Massachusetts*

1900. Waldo Lincoln, *Worcester, Massachusetts*

1902. John Lawrence Mauran, *St. Louis, Missouri*

1893. John Stewart McLennan, *Sidney, Cape Breton Island*

1904. Thomas Mott Osborne, *Auburn, New York*

1910. Ralph Delahaye Paine, *Durham, New Hampshire*

# List of Members

1893. Thomas Nelson Page, *Washington*

1902. Herbert Parker, *Lancaster, Massachusetts*

1884. Arthur Jeffrey Parsons, *Washington*

1900. Henry Smith Pritchett, *New York*

1895. Herbert Putnam, *Washington*

1904. Alexander Hamilton Rice, *London, England*

1886. Edward Robinson, *New York*

1884. Charles Edward Sampson, *New York*

1900. William F. Slocum, *Colorado Springs, Colorado*

1890. Francis Hopkinson Smith, *New York*

1892. Joseph Lindon Smith, *Dublin, New Hampshire*

1906. H. Morse Stephens, *San Francisco, California*

1908. Bellamy Storer, *Cincinnati, Ohio*

1894. Douglas Hamilton Thomas, Jr., *Baltimore, Maryland*

1904. Charles Harrison Tweed, *New York*

# The Tavern Club

1893. William Austin Wadsworth, *Geneseo, New York*

1893. Theodore Wendel, *Ipswich, Massachusetts*

1886. William Johnson Winch, *Windsor, Vermont*

1884. Owen Wister, *Philadelphia, Pennsylvania*

1893. Henry Roger Wolcott, *New York*

## Honorary Members

1897. Thomas Bailey Aldrich. 1907
1884. Henry Pickering Bowditch. 1911
1902. Le Barron Russell Briggs
1885. Martin Brimmer. 1896
1904. Charles William Eliot
1884. Wilhelm Gericke
1884. Henry Lee Higginson
1896. Adams Sherman Hill. 1910
1889. Oliver Wendell Holmes. 1894
1894. Oliver Wendell Holmes
1884. William Dean Howells
1911. Henry James
1908. William James. 1910
1888. Henry Lee. 1889

32

# List of Members

1885. James Russell Lowell.   1891
1885. Charles Eliot Norton.   1908
1895. Ignace J. Paderewski
1890. John Singer Sargent
1903. Augustus St. Gaudens
1887. Charles Dudley Warner.   1900
1909. Leonard Wood

## Charter Members

Timothée Adamowski
Robert Day Andrews
William Payne Blake
William Norton Bullard
Edward Burnett
Sigourney Butler
Frederic Crowninshield
Elbridge Gerry Cutler
Arthur Edward Davis
Edward Kellogg Dunham
Henry Strong Durand
Thomas Carey Felton
Reginald Heber Fitz
James Goldthwaite Freeman
Ignaz Marcel Gaugengigl
Francis Boott Greenough

# The Tavern Club

George Griswold Hayward
Clyde Du Vernet Hunt
Herbert Jaques
Samuel Wood Langmaid
Elliot Cabot Lee
Francis Wilson Lee
John Torrey Linzee
John Dandridge Henley Luce
John Hildreth McCollum
George Chickering Munzig
Arthur Jeffrey Parsons
Benjamin Curtis Porter
Morton Prince
Henry Parker Quincy
William Lambert Richardson
Arthur Rotch
Charles Edward Sampson
Joshua Montgomery Sears
Henry Harrison Sprague
George Stedman
Charles Wilkins Sturgis
Francis Shaw Sturgis
Thomas Russell Sullivan
Henry Walton Swift
George Horton Tilden
George Baxter Upham

# List of Members

Frederic Porter Vinton
Francis Sedgwick Watson
William Fletcher Weld
John Tyler Wheelwright
Royal Whitman
O--en Wister

# Former Officers of the Club

## 1884

### PRESIDENT

William Dean Howells

### SECRETARY

William Norton Bullard

### TREASURER

John Dandridge Henley Luce

### DIRECTORS

William Payne Blake, *Chairman*
Edward Burnett
George Chickering Munzig
Arthur Rotch

# The Tavern Club

George Horton Tilden
Francis Sedgwick Watson
Royal Whitman

### ELECTION COMMITTEE

Elbridge Gerry Cutler
Francis Wilson Lee
Benjamin Curtis Porter
Henry Harrison Sprague
Thomas Russell Sullivan
George Horton Tilden

### HOUSE COMMITTEE

George Chickering Munzig
Francis Sedgwick Watson
George Horton Tilden

## 1885

### PRESIDENT

William Dean Howells

### SECRETARY

George Howard Monks

### TREASURER

John Dandridge Henley Luce

# List of Members

37

# The Tavern Club

### SECRETARY

George Howard Monks

### TREASURER

John Dandridge Henley Luce

### DIRECTORS

Timothée Adamowski
William Payne Blake, *Chairman*
Herbert Jaques
George Chickering Munzig
George Horton Tilden
Joseph Weatherhead Warren

### ELECTION COMMITTEE

William Norton Bullard
Francis Wilson Lee
Benjamin Curtis Porter
Henry Harrison Sprague
George Horton Tilden
Francis Sedgwick Watson

### HOUSE COMMITTEE

George Chickering Munzig
George Horton Tilden
Herbert Jaques

# List of Members

1887

## PRESIDENT
William Dean Howells

## VICE-PRESIDENTS
Charles Eliot Norton
Henry Munroe Rogers

## SECRETARY
George Howard Monks

## TREASURER
John Dandridge Henley Luce

## DIRECTORS
William Payne Blake, *Chairman*
Herbert Jaques
George Chickering Munzig
Charles Edward Sampson
George Horton Tilden
Joseph Weatherhead Warren

## ELECTION COMMITTEE
William Norton Bullard
Francis Wilson Lee
Henry Harrison Sprague
Thomas Russell Sullivan
George Horton Tilden
Francis Sedgwick Watson

# The Tavern Club

## HOUSE COMMITTEE

William Payne Blake
George Chickering Munzig
George Horton Tilden
Charles Edward Sampson
Joseph Weatherhead Warren

### 1888

#### PRESIDENT

Henry Lee

#### VICE-PRESIDENTS

Charles Eliot Norton
Henry Munroe Rogers

#### SECRETARY

George Howard Monks

#### TREASURER

John Dandridge Henley Luce

#### DIRECTORS

William Payne Blake, *Chairman*
Augustus Hemenway
Henry Lee Morse
Charles Edward Sampson
George Horton Tilden
Joseph Weatherhead Warren

# List of Members

41

# The Tavern Club

# List of Members

43

# The Tavern Club

**VICE-PRESIDENTS**

Martin Brimmer

Henry Munroe Rogers

**SECRETARY**

Isidore Braggiotti

**TREASURER**

John Dandridge Henley Luce

**DIRECTORS**

William Payne Blake, *Chairman*

Augustus Hemenway

George Howard Monks

Henry Lee Morse

Charles Edward Sampson

Francis Shaw Sturgis

**ELECTION COMMITTEE**

Vincent Yardley Bowditch

Arthur Astor Carey

Francis Boott Greenough

Clayton Johns

Edward Robinson

Henry Harrison Sprague

**HOUSE COMMITTEE**

The Directors

# List of Members

## 1892

### PRESIDENT
Charles Eliot Norton

### VICE-PRESIDENTS
Martin Brimmer
Henry Munroe Rogers

### SECRETARY
George Baxter Upham

### TREASURER
Francis Wilson Lee

### DIRECTORS
William Payne Blake, *Chairman*
Augustus Hemenway
George Howard Monks
Henry Lee Morse
Charles Edward Sampson

### ELECTION COMMITTEE
Vincent Yardley Bowditch
Isadore Braggiotti
Arthur Astor Carey
John Templeman Coolidge, Jr.
Francis Boott Greenough
Clayton Johns

# The Tavern Club

HOUSE COMMITTEE

The Directors

## 1893

PRESIDENT

Charles Eliot Norton

VICE-PRESIDENTS

Martin Brimmer
Henry Munroe Rogers

SECRETARY

George Baxter Upham

TREASURER

Francis Wilson Lee

DIRECTORS

William Payne Blake, *Chairman*
Augustus Hemenway
George Howard Monks
Henry Lee Morse
Franz Eduard Zerrahn
Francis Shaw Sturgis

ELECTION COMMITTEE

William Sturgis Bigelow
Isidore Braggiotti
Arthur Astor Carey

46

# List of Members

John Templeman Coolidge, Jr.
Francis Boott Greenough
Barrett Wendell

### HOUSE COMMITTEE
The Directors

## 1894

### PRESIDENT
Charles Eliot Norton

### VICE-PRESIDENTS
Martin Brimmer
Henry Munroe Rogers

### SECRETARY
George Baxter Upham

### TREASURER
Francis Wilson Lee

### DIRECTORS
William Payne Blake, *Chairman*
Arlo Bates
Augustus Hemenway
Herbert Jaques
George Howard Monks
Franz Eduard Zerrahn

# The Tavern Club

### ELECTION COMMITTEE

George Pierce Baker
William Sturgis Bigelow
John Templeman Coolidge, Jr.
John Cummings Munro
Francis Shaw Sturgis
Thomas Russell Sullivan

### HOUSE COMMITTEE

The Directors

## 1895

### PRESIDENT

Charles Eliot Norton

### VICE-PRESIDENTS

Martin Brimmer
Henry Munroe Rogers

### SECRETARY

George Baxter Upham

### TREASURER

Francis Wilson Lee

### DIRECTORS

William Payne Blake, *Chairman*
Arlo Bates
Joseph Smith Bigelow

# List of Members

Augustus Hemenway
Josiah Byram Millet
Franz Eduard Zerrahn

### ELECTION COMMITTEE

George Pierce Baker
William Sturgis Bigelow
Mathew Luce, Jr.
John Cummings Munro
Francis Shaw Sturgis
Thomas Russell Sullivan

### HOUSE COMMITTEE

The Directors

## 1896

### PRESIDENT

Charles Eliot Norton

### VICE-PRESIDENTS

Martin Brimmer
Henry Munroe Rogers

### SECRETARY

George Baxter Upham

### TREASURER

Horatio Appleton Lamb

49

# The Tavern Club

## DIRECTORS

William Payne Blake, *Chairman*
Joseph Smith Bigelow
Herbert Leslie Burrell
Augustus Hemenway
Josiah Byram Millet
Franz Eduard Zerrahn

## ELECTION COMMITTEE

George Pierce Baker
Vincent Yardley Bowditch
Harry Burnett
Stephen Van Rensselaer Crosby
Mathew Luce, Jr.
John Cummings Munro

## HOUSE COMMITTEE

The Directors

## 1897

### PRESIDENT

Charles Eliot Norton

### VICE-PRESIDENTS

Henry Lee Higginson
Henry Munroe Rogers

# List of Members

# The Tavern Club

### VICE-PRESIDENTS

Henry Lee Higginson
Henry Munroe Rogers

### SECRETARY

Herbert Putnam

### TREASURER

Harry Burnett

### DIRECTORS

William Payne Blake, *Chairman*
Joseph Smith Bigelow
Herbert Leslie Burrell
Augustus Hemenway
Josiah Byram Millet
Franz Eduard Zerrahn

### ELECTION COMMITTEE

Holker Abbott
Winthrop Ames
Vincent Yardley Bowditch
Edward Robinson
Charles Russell Sturgis
George Baxter Upham

### HOUSE COMMITTEE

The Directors

# List of Members

## 1899

53

# The Tavern Club

Edward Robinson
Charles Russell Sturgis
George Baxter Upham

### HOUSE COMMITTEE
The Directors

## 1900

### PRESIDENT
Henry Lee Higginson

### VICE-PRESIDENTS
Henry Munroe Rogers
Oliver Wendell Holmes

### SECRETARY
Lorin Fuller Deland

### TREASURER
Harry Burnett

### DIRECTORS
Frank Weston Benson
Henry Forbes Bigelow
Robert Homans
Josiah Byram Millet
George Baxter Upham, *Chairman*
Franz Eduard Zerrahn

54

# List of Members

# The Tavern Club

Herbert Jaques
Josiah Byram Millet
George Baxter Upham, *Chairman*

### ELECTION COMMITTEE

Franklin Greene Balch
George Edward Barton
Charles Ayer Clough
Robert Homans
Alexander Wadsworth Longfellow
Paul Thorndike

### HOUSE COMMITTEE

The Directors

## 1902

### PRESIDENT

Henry Lee Higginson

### VICE-PRESIDENTS

Oliver Wendell Holmes
Adams Sherman Hill

### SECRETARY

Holker Abbott

### TREASURER

Charles Russell Sturgis

# List of Members

### DIRECTORS

Henry Forbes Bigelow
Mark Antony De Wolfe Howe
Guy Lowell
Frederic Jesup Stimson
Richard Clipston Sturgis
George Baxter Upham, *Chairman*

### ELECTION COMMITTEE

George Edward Barton
Charles Ayer Clough
Arthur Dehon Hill
Alexander Wadsworth Longfellow
Guy Murchie
Thomas Russell Sullivan

### HOUSE COMMITTEE

Guy Murchie, *Chairman*

## 1903

### PRESIDENT

Henry Lee Higginson

### VICE-PRESIDENTS

Adams Sherman Hill
Henry Pickering Bowditch

### SECRETARY

Holker Abbott

# The Tavern Club

58

# List of Members

### TREASURER

Charles Russell Sturgis

### DIRECTORS

Henry Forbes Bigelow
John Bapst Blake
Mark Antony De Wolfe Howe
Herbert Jaques
Richard Clipston Sturgis
George Baxter Upham, *Chairman*

### ELECTION COMMITTEE

Winthrop Ames
Arthur Dehon Hill
Clayton Johns
Guy Murchie
Arthur Stanwood Pier
Thomas Russell Sullivan

### HOUSE COMMITTEE

Guy Murchie, *Chairman*

## 1905

### PRESIDENT

Henry Lee Higginson

### VICE-PRESIDENTS

Adams Sherman Hill
Henry Pickering Bowditch

# The Tavern Club

### SECRETARY
Holker Abbott

### TREASURER
Charles Russell Sturgis

### DIRECTORS
Henry Forbes Bigelow
John Bapst Blake
Mark Antony De Wolfe Howe
Herbert Jaques
Richard Clipston Sturgis
George Baxter Upham, *Chairman*

### ELECTION COMMITTEE
Holker Abbott
Winthrop Ames
Clayton Johns
Alexander Wadsworth Longfellow
Henry Leyman
Guy Murchie
Arthur Stanwood Pier
Francis Shaw Sturgis
Paul Thorndike
Henry Vaughan

### HOUSE COMMITTEE
Guy Murchie, *Chairman*

# List of Members

## 1906

### PRESIDENT
Henry Lee Higginson

### VICE-PRESIDENTS
Adams Sherman Hill
Henry Pickering Bowditch

### SECRETARY
Holker Abbott

### TREASURER
Charles Russell Sturgis

### DIRECTORS
Henry Forbes Bigelow
John Bapst Blake
Mark Antony De Wolfe Howe
Herbert Jaques
Richard Clipston Sturgis
George Baxter Upham

### ELECTION COMMITTEE
Holker Abbott
Walter Channing Bailey
Frank Weston Benson
Frederick Shepherd Converse

# The Tavern Club

Alexander Wadsworth Longfellow
Henry Lyman
Francis Shaw Sturgis
Paul Thorndike
Henry Vaughan

### HOUSE COMMITTEE

Guy Murchie

## 1907

### PRESIDENT

Henry Lee Higginson

### VICE-PRESIDENTS

Henry Pickering Bowditch
Abbott Lawrence Lowell

### SECRETARY

Holker Abbott

### TREASURER

Charles Russell Sturgis

### DIRECTORS

Henry Forbes Bigelow
John Bapst Blake
Mark Antony De Wolfe Howe

# List of Members

Herbert Jaques
Richard Clipston Sturgis
George Baxter Upham

### ELECTION COMMITTEE

Holker Abbott
Walter Channing Bailey
Frank Weston Benson
Frederick Shepherd Converse
Alexander Wadsworth Longfellow
William Samuel Patten
Jeremiah Smith, Jr.
Francis Shaw Sturgis
Paul Thorndike
Edward Ross Warren

### HOUSE COMMITTEE

Guy Murchie

## 1908

### PRESIDENT

Henry Lee Higginson

### VICE-PRESIDENTS

Thomas Russell Sullivan
Abbott Lawrence Lowell

# The Tavern Club

# List of Members

# The Tavern Club

William Samuel Patten
Bliss Perry
Jeremiah Smith, Jr.
Edmund Charles Tarbell
Edward Ross Warren

### HOUSE COMMITTEE

Guy Murchie

## 1910

### PRESIDENT

Henry Lee Higginson

### VICE-PRESIDENTS

Arlo Bates
John Bapst Blake

### SECRETARY

Holker Abbott

### TREASURER

Henry Goodwin Vaughan

### DIRECTORS

Walter Channing Bailey
William James
Mark Antony De Wolfe Howe
Arthur Stanwood Pier

# List of Members

Richard Clipston Sturgis
George Baxter Upham

## ELECTION COMMITTEE

Holker Abbott
Samuel Cabot
Charles Kimball Cummings
Francis Henry Davenport
Charles Stewart Forbes
Guy Lowell
Henry Lyman
Edmund Charles Tarbell
Eliot Wadsworth
Langdon Warner

## HOUSE COMMITTEE

Guy Murchie

## 1911

### PRESIDENT

Henry Lee Higginson

### VICE-PRESIDENTS

Arlo Bates
Robert Grant

### SECRETARY

Holker Abbott

# The Tavern Club

**TREASURER**

Henry Goodwin Vaughan

**DIRECTORS**

Walter Channing Bailey
Charles Kimball Cummings
John Wheelock Elliott
William James
William Stanley Parker
Arthur Stanwood Pier
George Baxter Upham

**ELECTION COMMITTEE**

Holker Abbott
Samuel Cabot
Charles Stewart Forbes
Mark Antony De Wolfe Howe
Guy Lowell
Edmund Charles Tarbell
Paul Thorndike
Eliot Wadsworth
Langdon Warner
Arthur Henry Weed

**HOUSE COMMITTEE**

Guy Murchie
Charles Stewart Forbes
Paul Thorndike

68

𝔓rinteꝺ, with decorations drawn by
F. G. Attwood, from designs of
D. B. Updike, at the Univer-
sity Press, Cambridge,
September first
MCMXI